The Credit Cure

$100k in Credit Within 60 Days:
Repair Your Past and Build Your Future

By Landys 101

ISBN: 9798329993080

DEDICATION

This book is dedicated to all the aspiring entrepreneurs and small business owners who dare to dream big and strive for success. May you find inspiration, guidance, and empowerment within these pages as you embark on your journey to master the art of business credit. Your dedication, resilience, and passion are the driving forces behind innovation and progress, and it is with great admiration and respect that I dedicate this book to you. May your entrepreneurial spirit continue to flourish, and may you achieve all your aspirations and goals.

CONTENTS

ACKNOWLEDGMENTS

To My family and friends: Their unwavering support and encouragement throughout this project were invaluable. Their belief in my vision fueled my motivation and perseverance. My sincere appreciation goes to my editor, whose keen eye and insightful feedback significantly improved the clarity, focus, and overall impact of the manuscript. I am particularly grateful to my mentors for their willingness to share their expertise and provide valuable feedback on the financial concepts presented in this book. Their insights ensured the accuracy and comprehensiveness of the content. To the dedicated members of The Credit Cure community who bravely shared their stories and struggles, thank you. Your experiences were a constant source of inspiration and a powerful reminder of the transformative impact of financial wellness.

In conclusion, I extend my heartfelt gratitude to the readers. Embarking on a journey towards financial empowerment requires courage and commitment. I trust that The Credit Cure equips you with the knowledge and actionable strategies necessary to achieve your credit cure goals and build a secure financial future.

The Credit Cure

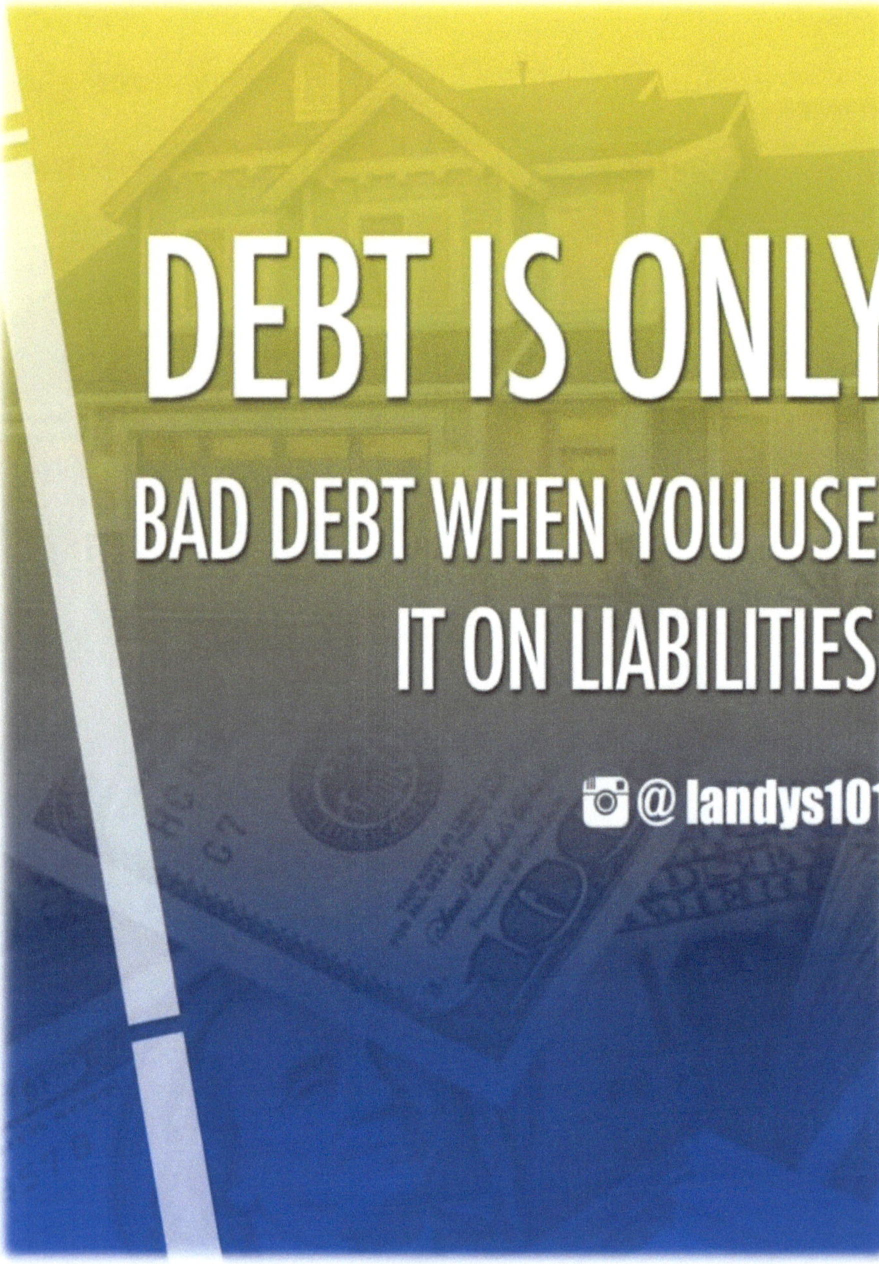
DEBT IS ONLY
BAD DEBT WHEN YOU USE
IT ON LIABILITIES
@ landys101

Understanding Business Credit

The obvious fact of the matter is leveraging credit to start businesses, fund projects, and buy properties are things people have been doing for hundreds of years but because of NON-ECONOMICAL curriculum in the school systems and some of our elders who are scared of credit is the reason why we are limited to this knowledge. Just for one second think of the big buildings downtown or even shopping malls. Do you honestly think that someone is paying 100% cash for these? The answer is 100% NO and YES, these buildings and malls have been around for years which goes back to my original statement that this has been going on for a long time!

In this book I would like to not only show you how get access to large lines of credit but also show you exactly where to go to apply for the credit. A few things you can expect to learn from this book.

1. How to structure your credit report to get approved for large lines of credit

2. How to apply for these credit cards/ Lines of Credit and what to put on applications

3. How to apply for multiple cards and lines of Credit with limited inquires on your report

4. How to work the system in the banks to get line increases on those cards

5. The list of banks that offer over 10k in credit lines/Credit card along with the credit bureau they pull from.

6. What is the difference between credit cards and lines of credit

7. What key terms to look for on Credit cards

8. How to transfer the money off the credit cards into your checking account to use for real estate purchases.

Notes

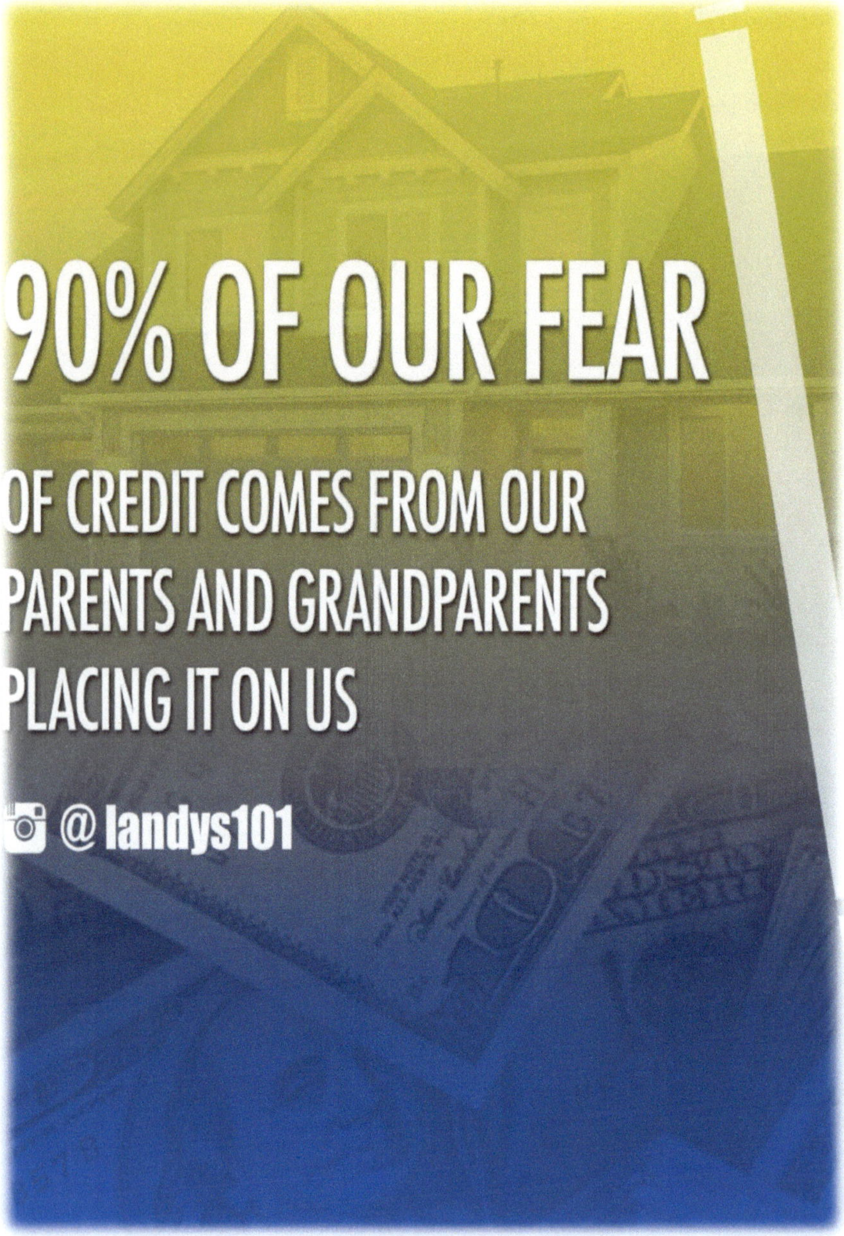
90% OF OUR FEAR
OF CREDIT COMES FROM OUR
PARENTS AND GRANDPARENTS
PLACING IT ON US
@landys101

STRUCTURING YOUR CREDIT REPORT

Structuring your credit report is the most important piece to this 100k credit formula.

Without having a solid credit report, you are either denied or are super limited to the amount of funding you will receive.

The Key things you want to have in order on your credit report are listed below:

DEROGATORY MARKS: You want to make sure you do not have any derogatory remarks on your credit report such as collections and late payments. A company you can work with that can get them removed is as little as 24hrs IS.
HTTPS://WWW.INSTAGRAM.COM/LANDYS101/

HIGH UTILIZATION: utilization is the amount of money owed on your credit card/Line of your attitude is under 30% which means if your max limit is $10,000 then you shouldn't spend over $3,000. Why this is a negative to you because the banks now will look at you as if you are relying on your credit to survive. You never want the banks to look at you as in you need credit.

INQUIRIES: Inquiries are notifications on your credit report that show when someone did a hard pull on your credit. Why this can negatively affect you is

for funding you should investigate removing some of your inquiries to a very limited amount (under 3 or 4). You can call the credit bureaus and ask for those inquiries to be removed.

LATE PAYMENTS: Late payments are a huge factor in being approved for funding. The reason why late payments are a big factor is because the banks will simply believe that "if you cannot pay the other company on time then you will not pay us back on time". One thing that you can do that is simple and does not require serious credit repair is call the company and ask for a forgiveness.

PRIMARY LINES: Primary lines are credit cards, lines of credit, loans, car notes, mortgages, etc., that you are listed as the primary person for those accounts. why is this so important is because the new banks will see that you are already used to having credit and hopefully responsible with the credit. The truth that people may not know is that even with a perfect credit score you can still be you are approved for with the new banks. This means if you already have a 5k-10k account then the new bank will most likely match and/or be in the same ballpark also, there are other companies that offer lines of credit openly like **ikamanagement.info** that can provide a $5,000 line with their company that will report on your account.

QUICK GEM When going to my jewelers club you will have to purchase something for at least $100. When going to check out they will ask do you want to apply for credit to pay for instead and get up to $5,000 in financing. Click apply and complete short APPLICATION (what credit score you have does not matter). Once completed you will be awarded the $5,000 credit limit and be asked to pay only half of the money for the item you chose along with a onetime $100 fee. Now that $5000 account will report on your credit. Please make sure you pay the remaining balance for the time you purchased.

QUICK GEM make sure you remove any fraud alerts that may be on your account. You can simply call the bureau and ask them to remove. This will delay the approval process for you if you have an open fraud alert

Notes

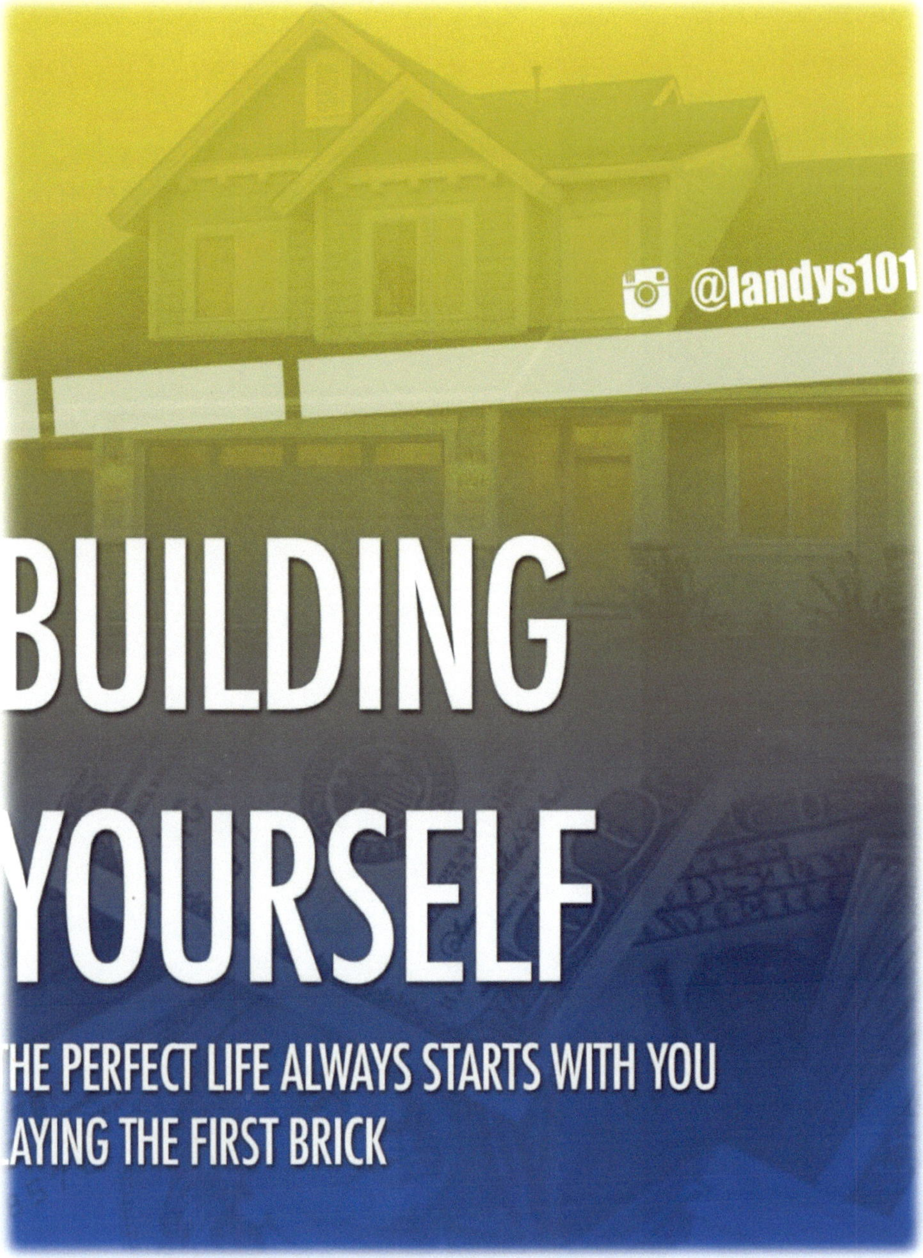
@landys101
BUILDING
YOURSELF
THE PERFECT LIFE ALWAYS STARTS WITH YOU
LAYING THE FIRST BRICK

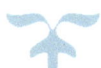

APPLYING FOR CREDIT

Now when applying for credit you want to be very strategic, so you get results!! As you know you can simply go online and put in an application, right? Pretty simple. However, when you want to get access to larger funding and just overall get approved you want to set things up a little more on purpose instead of just leaving it up to chance. In this section I will be showing you several steps that you should take prior to submitting any application for funding.

BUILDING A RELATIONSHIP

I want you to completely understand that building relationships in every aspect of your life is more important than money. Building a relationship first with someone who can lead you to more money than you originally imagined. That same concept works with banks!!

Building a relationship with a bank will allow you to get looked at a lot better than someone who does not have a relationship with that bank. This relationship bonus leads to credit application approvals and higher limits on your credit cards and/or lines of credit.

FULL DISCLOSURE you can get approved for funding without opening an account however it does help.

Now what does building a relationship mean?

What I mean by building a relationship with a bank is simply opening a checking and savings account with them and depositing some money into the account. The money doesn't have to be thousands of dollars but simply whatever their minimum requirement is. Most banks require a $, $25, or $50 deposit in order to open an account with them. Personally, I always just put a little bit more than the minimum in the account. So, for example if the minimum is $25 I go ahead and put $20-$50 in to start with instead. What happens is I am going over the bare minimum to get involved with them, but I also am over all the other accounts that are over drafted, zero balance, and bare minimum balance. This will reflect good on me and help with building that relationship. Now the next thing that I personally do which helps with me is wait 30-60 days before actually applying. *Full disclosure* You can apply the first or second day of you opening an account however I have noticed with myself and friends that the accounts opened longer get approved for more.

Also remember when applying on the first day and not receiving the max credit line you can always ask for a line increase within 60-90 days of receiving the card.

Quick Gem when receiving a credit card and looking to get a line increase in the next 60-90 days you should spend up to 30% on the card and then pay it off before the due date on the card. What happens is this will show not only usage on the card but also responsibility with the credit card

because you are not going over and/or holding a balance over 30% of its utilization. What you can also do is buy visa gift cards with that credit card and then utilize the same gift card to pay back the credit card balance. Not only are you building a relationship but if the bank offers reward points you will be receiving those as well.

WITH LEVERAGING CREDIT

YOU COULD BUY 10 HOUSES WITH THE PRICE OF ONE.

@landys101

UNDERSTANDING THE APPROVAL CONDITIONS

So, in this step you will be looking for the most important information and that is "what are the conditions that the bank is looking for."

So, every bank looks for different things in order to approve an application. A certain credit score, amount of money, etc. These are things you want to know before applying that way you can identify if it is worth you applying to now or later. Also, one very important thing you need to know what credit bureau they pull from. So, you have 3 credit bureaus that banks most commonly pull from which are Experian, Equifax, and Transunion. As you may know already each one shows a different score for your personal credit. Now why is this so important to know is because when you are applying for a bank that pulls from Experian and you know that you have 2 collections on your Experian account but not on your Transunion account then it may not be best to apply for that bank just yet. Also, if you apply for 3 different banks and each bank pulls from a different bureau then you can essentially apply for all 3 banks with just one hard inquiry on each report!

You are probably wondering how can I find out this information about banks and who they pull from? One quick way is when you are opening the account to begin with you can ask the representative handling your new account those questions.

Ex: "Hey thanks for opening up my account! Just a quick question? If I one day in the future was curious about lending options with you guys' what type of requirements need to be met in order to get approved? As far as minimum credit score, income, or if the account needs to be opened for a certain amount of time? also, who do you guys usually pull from as far as credit bureau?"

This question may sound abrasive to you however as the bank representative it their job to answer all questions especially for brand new members. You can also use this approach.

Ex: " HEY WHAT CREDIT BUREAU DO YOU GUYS PULL FROM BECAUSE MY CREDIT IS LOCKED, AND I NEED TO KNOW WHICH ONE TO UNLOCK BEFORE APPLYING SO I WON'T CREATE ANY ISSUES OR DELAYS ON YOUR END"

THIS ONE PERSONALLY ALWAYS WORKS FOR ME ALL THE TIME.

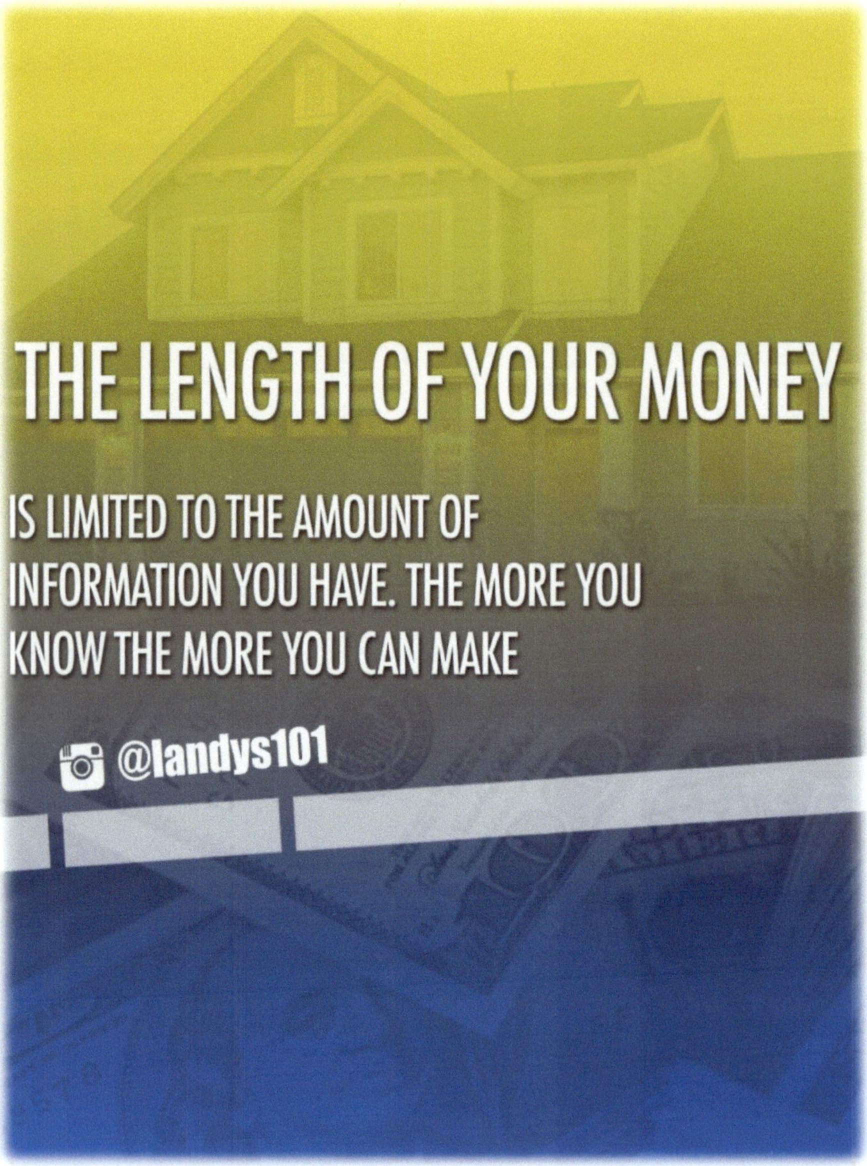
THE LENGTH OF YOUR MONEY
IS LIMITED TO THE AMOUNT OF INFORMATION YOU HAVE. THE MORE YOU KNOW THE MORE YOU CAN MAKE
@landys101

WHICH CARDS TO APPLY FOR

Most banks and credit card companies offer a vast variety of cards which often leave you confused on which one to apply for. I highly recommend applying for cards based on what we are using the money for (Real estate). I love 0% interest cards for 12 months or more. What does that mean? So, over the next 12 months any money that you spend on that credit card is the only amount you must pay back if paid within 12 months and no interest! So essentially the bank is lending you money for free!

Example: You are approved for $1,000 and spend $1,000 now you are only obligated to pay back that exact $1,000 if done within 12 MONTHS (or whatever the terms are).

Also, another thing to look for when picking cards are cash rewards cards. This means they offer you cash back or reward points when you spend with that card so, you can receive hundreds or maybe even thousands back by just buying everyday purchases that you normally would pay for with cash or debit card.

Lastly check and see if a card has a signing bonus. A signing bonus is a reward of points, credits, or cash to you just for getting approved for the card.

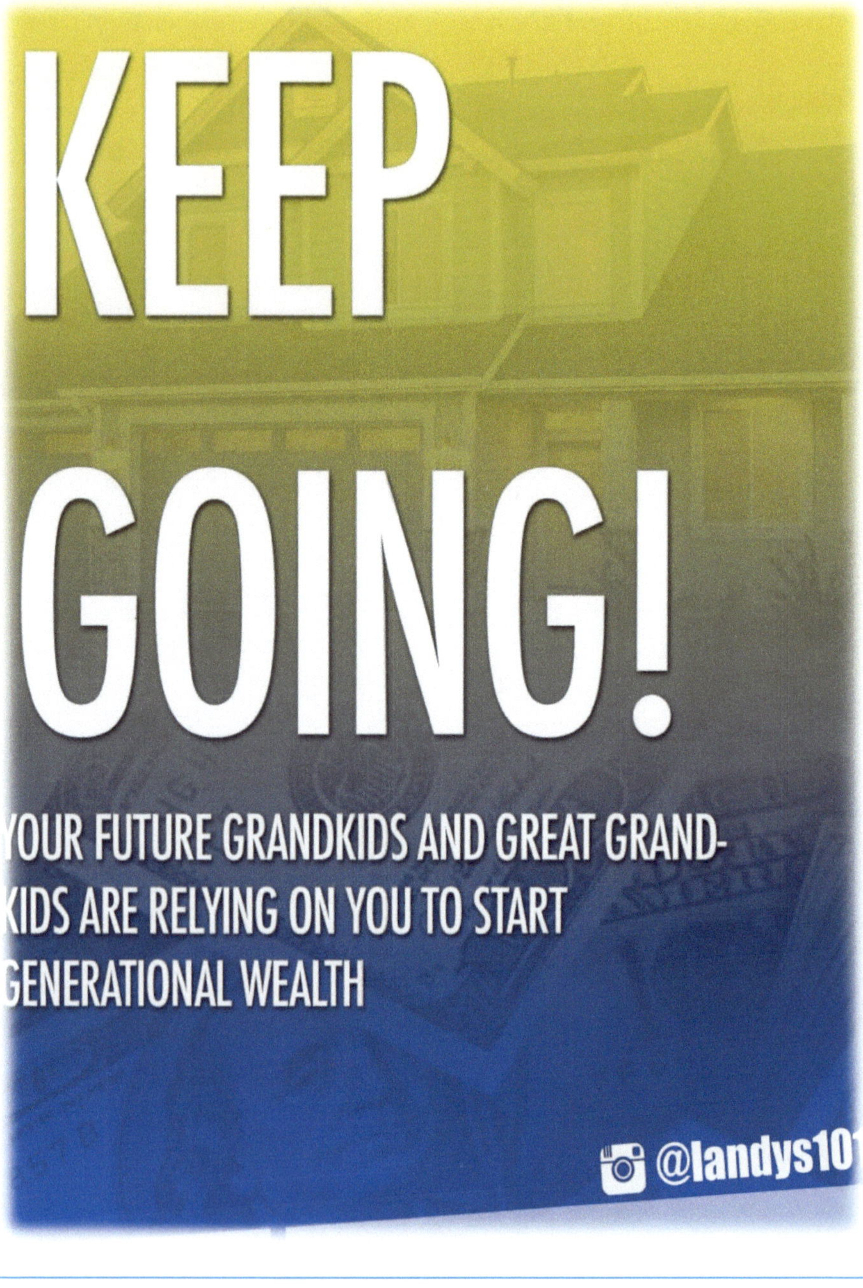
KEEP
GOING!
YOUR FUTURE GRANDKIDS AND GREAT GRAND-
KIDS ARE RELYING ON YOU TO START
GENERATIONAL WEALTH
@landys101

WHAT TO PUT ON THE APPLICATION

Ok great so now you have a relationship with a bank and are ready to go for funding. What I totally recommend doing is applying for the application online rather than going into the branch. This is because you are now able to apply for multiple credit cards at one time from your computer rather than trying to drive from bank to bank. also, when you apply at one time the other banks will not see each other's inquiries!

When applying for your credit cards there are a couple things that you want to have on the application. When it comes down to your income always put more than what you make I.e., double or triple the amount. So, for example if you make 50k a year put down 100k-150k as your income. When applying for credit cards with $50k or under limits they do not require documentation such as tax returns or pay stubs. Any unsecured credit that you apply for over $50k they will request documentation. Banks and credit card companies approve you based on your credit profile and your income. These things go hand and hand especially in order to receive higher limits.

Another thing to note when applying is the time you submit. Personally, I realized that the earlier I submit the application the faster the approval. So, for example when I apply at 9am with a bank | received an approval instantly or within the hour. Applying later in the day when the loan department is closing will lead to your application to be pushed back.

Quick Gem for some banks like navy Federal credit union when you apply after 2am you have an extremely higher chance to get approved and approved for a higher limit. At this point you tap into their automated system and the computer automatically approves the application without a person to overview.

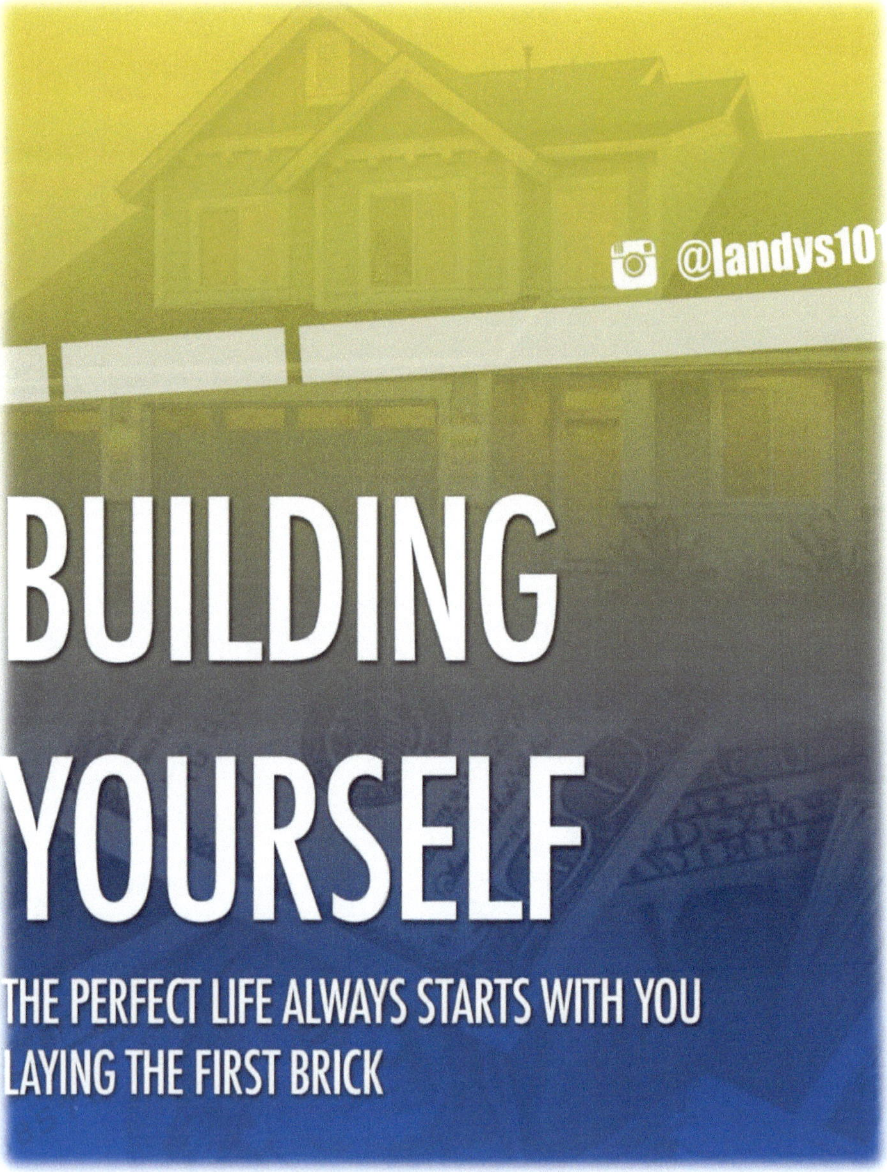

BUILDING YOURSELF

THE PERFECT LIFE ALWAYS STARTS WITH YOU LAYING THE FIRST BRICK

@landys101